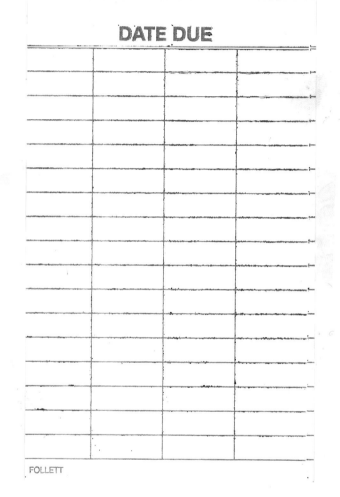

DATE DUE

FOLLETT

3.6/0.5

From Puppy to Dog

Following the Life Cycle

by Suzanne Slade

illustrated by Jeff Yesh

PICTURE WINDOW BOOKS
Minneapolis, Minnesota

Thanks to our advisers for their expertise:

Dr. Julie Berndt, D.V.M.
Minnesota Valley Pet Hospital
Mankato, Minnesota

Terry Flaherty, Ph.D., Professor of English
Minnesota State University, Mankato

Editor: Shelly Lyons
Designers: Nathan Gassman and Lori Bye
Page Production: Melissa Kes
Associate Managing Editor: Christianne Jones
The illustrations in this book were created digitally.

Photo Credits: © Phil Date/Shutterstock, 23.

Picture Window Books
1710 Roe Crest Drive
North Mankato, Minnesota 56003
www.picturewindowbooks.com

Library of Congress Cataloging-in-Publication Data
Slade, Suzanne.
From puppy to dog : following the life cycle / by Suzanne Slade ;
illustrated by Jeff Yesh.
p. cm. — (Amazing science: life cycle)
Includes index.
ISBN-13: 978-1-4048-4928-0 (library binding)
1. Dogs—Life cycles—Juvenile literature.
I. Yesh, Jeff, 1971- ill. II. Title.
SF426.5.S575 2009
636.7—dc22   2008006434

Printed in the United States of America
in Stevens Point, Wisconsin.
072013   007593R

Table of Contents

Furry Friends

There are many different kinds of dogs in the world. Some dogs do jobs that help people. Other dogs make great friends. It's exciting to watch a puppy grow into a dog. During its life cycle, a dog changes in many ways. Let's take a closer look at the life cycle of a popular pet—the golden retriever.

There are more than 60 million pet dogs in the United States.

A Litter Is Born

A puppy grows inside of its mother for nine weeks before it is born. This is called the gestation period. When a mother is ready to give birth, she looks for a safe place to have her puppies. There are usually eight puppies in a litter of golden retrievers. A litter is a group of baby animals that are born at one time to the same mother.

Different breeds, or kinds of dogs, have different sizes of litters. For example, beagles have five to seven puppies in a litter. Tiny Yorkshire terriers usually have a litter of only three puppies.

Newborn Puppy

A newborn puppy is helpless. It cannot see or hear because its eyes and ears are closed. But a new puppy's nose works well. A puppy stays near the smell of its mother and her milk.

A puppy is born with soft fur called a "puppy coat."
The puppy does not shed, or lose, this fur.

Mother's Milk

Young puppies spend most of their time sleeping and eating. Puppies suckle, or drink milk, from their mother. Milk is their only food for the first three weeks. A mother's milk has everything her puppies need to grow.

Newborn puppies spend about 30 percent of their time suckling. Some may drink as often as every 20 minutes.

Seeing the World

About 10 days after birth, a puppy's eyes begin to open. At first, things look fuzzy. The puppy's ears open about three days later. Then it can see and hear.

A puppy weighs twice its birth weight by the time it is 8 to 10 days old.

Stepping Out

Puppies start to walk when they are 2 to 3 weeks old. Puppies are very curious. They step out on shaky legs to explore the world around them. Young puppies also like to play, but they get tired easily. Puppies often gather together in a pile for a nap.

Socialization happens when puppies are 4 to 7 weeks old. During this time, puppies learn how to act around people and other dogs.

A New Home

Before a puppy can leave its mother, it must be weaned. This means the puppy doesn't drink milk from its mother anymore. Once a puppy is weaned, it can chew solid food and lap water from a dish. A golden retriever puppy is ready to leave its mother when it is 8 weeks old. Then the puppy may go to a new owner who will feed and care for it.

When a puppy is 3 weeks old, its baby teeth appear. As a puppy gets older, its tiny baby teeth begin to fall out. To help a puppy's new, larger teeth break through the gums, an owner may give it chew toys.

Starting the Cycle Again

Around its first birthday, a golden retriever puppy is considered an adult dog. Pet owners who would like their adult dog to mate should wait until the dog is 2 years old.

It is also important for the dog to be healthy before mating. After mating, new puppies begin growing inside the female. In just nine weeks, a new litter is born.

Most pet owners have their dog spayed or neutered. Female dogs are spayed, while male dogs are neutered. After having this operation, a dog cannot make puppies.

Slowing Down

Near the end of its life cycle, a golden retriever becomes less active. White hair often appears near its eyes and mouth. Although an older dog needs more rest, it is still a faithful and caring friend.

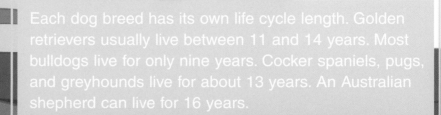

Each dog breed has its own life cycle length. Golden retrievers usually live between 11 and 14 years. Most bulldogs live for only nine years. Cocker spaniels, pugs, and greyhounds live for about 13 years. An Australian shepherd can live for 16 years.

Life Cycle of a Golden Retriever

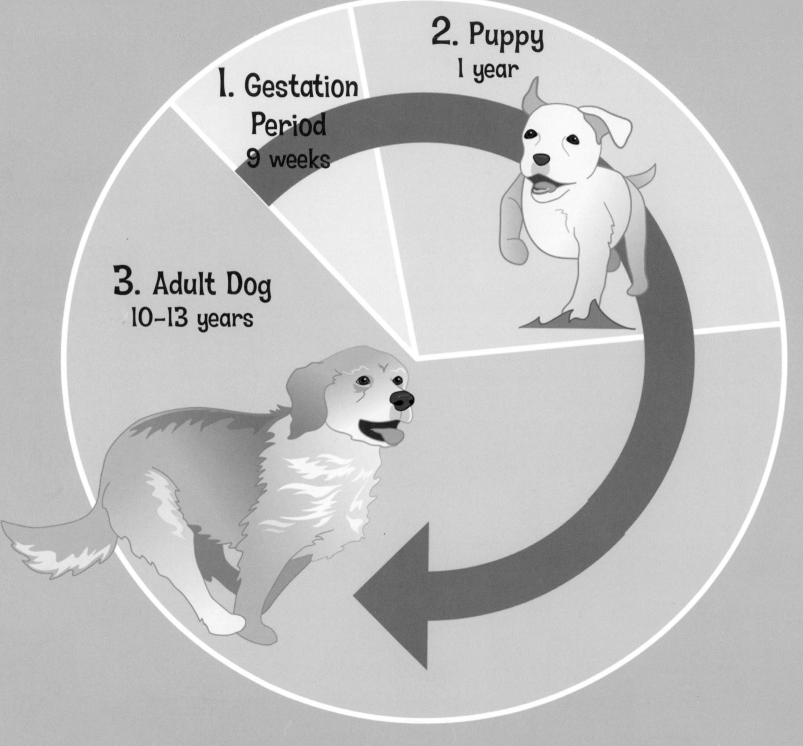

1. Gestation Period
9 weeks

2. Puppy
1 year

3. Adult Dog
10–13 years

Fun Facts

- Soon after a puppy is born, it can crawl forward. A puppy learns to crawl backward when it is about 15 to 18 days old.

- A puppy begins to wag its tail when it is 3 weeks old. Dogs wag their tails when they are happy or excited.

- The moisture on a dog's nose helps the dog smell things better. If a dog wants to follow a certain scent, it may lick its nose to improve its sense of smell.

- A basenji is the only kind of dog that cannot bark. This short-haired breed from Africa stands about 17 inches (43.2 centimeters) tall.

- Golden retrievers are good hunting dogs. They are also often trained to be guide dogs for the blind.

Adult golden retriever

Glossary

breed—a group of animals that look alike and are related to each other

gestation period—the amount of time an unborn animal spends inside its mother

litter—a group of animals born at the same time to one mother

mate—to join together to produce young

socialization—to learn to get along with animals and people

suckle—to drink milk from a mother

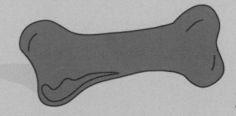

To Learn More

More Books to Read

Ganeri, Anita. *From Puppy to Dog.* Chicago: Heinemann Library, 2006.

Magloff, Lisa. *Puppy.* New York: DK Pub., 2005.

Tagliaferro, Linda. *Dogs and Their Puppies.* Mankato, Minn.: Capstone Press, 2004.

Trumbauer, Lisa. *The Life Cycle of a Dog.* Mankato, Minn.: Capstone Press, 2004

On the Web

FactHound offers a safe, fun way to find Web sites related to topics in this book.
All of the sites on FactHound have been researched by our staff.

1. Visit *www.facthound.com*
2. Type in this special code: 1404849289
3. Click on the FETCH IT button.

Your trusty FactHound will fetch the best sites for you!

Look for all of the books in the Amazing Science: Life Cycles series:

From Caterpillar to Butterfly: Following the Life Cycle
From Mealworm to Beetle: Following the Life Cycle
From Puppy to Dog: Following the Life Cycle
From Seed to Daisy: Following the Life Cycle
From Seed to Maple Tree: Following the Life Cycle
From Tadpole to Frog: Following the Life Cycle